Rookie
biographie

D0880554

Ronald Reagan

By Wil Mara

Consultant
Nanci R. Vargus, EdD
Assistant Professor of Literacy
University of Indianapolis
Indianapolis, Indiana

Children's Press®
A Division of Scholastic Inc.
New York   Toronto   London   Auckland   Sydney
Mexico City   New Delhi   Hong Kong
Danbury, Connecticut

Designer: Herman Adler Design
Photo Researcher: Caroline Anderson
The photo on the cover shows Ronald Reagan.

Library of Congress Cataloging-in-Publication Data

Mara, Wil.
  Ronald Reagan / by Wil Mara.
    p. cm. — (Rookie biographies)
  Includes index.
  ISBN 0-516-25271-2 (lib. bdg.)   0-516-25482-0 (pbk.)
  1. Reagan, Ronald—Juvenile literature. 2. Presidents—United States—
Biography—Juvenile literature. I. Title. II. Rookie biography.
  E877.M36 2005
  973.927'092—dc22   2005004030

4 5 6 7 8 9 10 R 14 13 12 11 10 09   62

Ronald Reagan was the 40th president of the United States.

He was born in Illinois in 1911. His family lived in a tiny apartment. They had very little money.

Reagan worked hard in school. He wanted a good education. He earned the money to go to college himself.

Ronald Reagan

People line up for free bread.

Reagan finished college in 1932. During this time, many people could not find work.

It was hard to buy food and clothes because people did not have much money.

Reagan stayed cheerful and hoped for the best. He went to California to work as an actor.

Ronald Reagan starred in many movies.

12

Reagan became interested
in politics while he was in
California. Politicians are people
who help run a community.

Reagan became the governor of California in 1967. A governor runs a whole state.

Many people liked Governor Reagan. They thought he should become president of the United States. He was elected president in 1980.

Reagan wanted people to feel hopeful about their country.

One way Reagan did this was to lower taxes. Taxes are money people pay to the government.

Reagan also made friends with Mikhail Gorbachev. Gorbachev was the leader of the Soviet Union.

The Soviet Union and America were enemies for many years. Reagan wanted the two countries to develop a better relationship.

Reagan made history by putting the first woman on the Supreme Court. The Supreme Court is the most powerful group of judges in America. This woman was Sandra Day O'Connor.

President Reagan and his wife Nancy board the president's plane.

Reagan's time as president ended in 1989. A few years later, he became sick with Alzheimer's disease. This disease affects the brain.

Reagan died on June 5, 2004.

He was 93 years old.

People admired Reagan because he was always cheerful about the future.

In 1994, Reagan wrote a last letter to the American people. In it he said, "I know that for America there will always be a bright dawn ahead."

Words You Know

actor

governor

Mikhail Gorbachev

president of the
United States

Sandra Day O'Connor

Index

About the Author

Wil Mara has written more than seventy books. He has written both fiction and nonfiction, for both children and adults.

Photo Credits

Photographs © 2005: AP/Wide World Photos: 24 (Rick Bowmer), 12 (GB), 7, 11, 15, 30 top; Corbis Images: 8 (Bettmann), 27 (James Glover II/Ventura County Star); Corbis Sygma/Eddie Adams: cover; Getty Images: 19, 28 (Dirck Halstead), 20, 30 bottom (David Hume Kennerly); Courtesy of Ronald Reagan Library: 3, 4, 16, 23, 31.